John Francis X. O'Conor

Cuneiform Text of a Recently Discovered Cylinder

of Nebuchadnezzar, King Of Babylon. From the original in the

Metropolitan Museum of Art, New York

John Francis X. O'Conor

Cuneiform Text of a Recently Discovered Cylinder
of Nebuchadnezzar, King Of Babylon. From the original in the Metropolitan Museum of Art, New York

ISBN/EAN: 9783337246280

Printed in Europe, USA, Canada, Australia, Japan

Cover: Foto ©ninafisch / pixelio.de

More available books at **www.hansebooks.com**

CUNEIFORM TEXT

OF A RECENTLY DISCOVERED

CYLINDER

OF

NEBUCHADNEZZAR II,

KING OF BABYLON

FROM THE ORIGINAL IN THE

METROPOLITAN MUSEUM OF ART

NEW YORK.

COPIED, TRANSLATED & PUBLISHED By
J. F. Xavier O'CONOR, S. J.

WOODSTOCK COLLEGE, MD.

———

WOODSTOCK COLLEGE
1885.

JOHN MURPHY & CO., PRINTERS.

BALTIMORE.

INDEX.

REFERENCES.

I R, II R, III R, IV R, V R = WAI. = Cuneiform Inscriptions of Western Asia. Sir Henry Rawlinson. The numerals before R, indicate the volume; after, the page. (London, 1861-70-75-80.) .

Del. Assyr. Lesestt. = Friedrich Delitzsch, Assyrische Lesestücke. (Leipzig, 1878.)

Del. Assyr. Stud. = Friedrich Delitzsch, Assyrische Studien. (Leipzig, 1874.)

Del. Wo lag das Paradies? = Friedrich Delitzsch. (Leipzig, 1881.)

ASKT. = Paul Haupt, Assyrische Sumerische Keilschrifttexte. (Leipzig, 1881-82.)

SFG. = Paul Haupt, Sumerische Familiengesetze. (Leipzig, 1879.)

BAL. = Paul Haupt, Beiträge zur Assyrischen Lautlehre. (1883.)

KAT. = Eberhard Schrader, Die Keilschriften und das Alte Testament. (Giessen, 1883.)

Neb. = Inscription Nebuchadnezzar, I R, 53-58.

Neb. Bab. = Cylinder-inscription from Babylon, I R, 51, No. 2.

Neb. Senk. = Cylinder-inscription Senkereh., I R, 51, No. 2.

Tig. I. Lotz = Tiglathpileser, I. Wm. Lotz. (Leipzig, 1880.)

Sarg. Cyl. = David G. Lyon, Keilschrifttexte Sargon's. (Leipzig, 1883.)

Menant. = Manuel de la langue Assyrienne. (Paris, 1880.)

AVAAW. = J. N. Strassmaier, S. J. Alphabetisches Verzeichniss der Assyrischen und Akkadischen Wörter. (Leipzig, 1882-83-84-85.)

ABVW. = J. N. Strassmaier, S. J. Altbabylonischen Verträge aus Warka. (Berlin, 1882.)

Cont. Tab. 17 Nab. = J. N. Strassmaier, S. J. Contract Tablet, 17th year of Nabonidus. (London, 1882.)

4

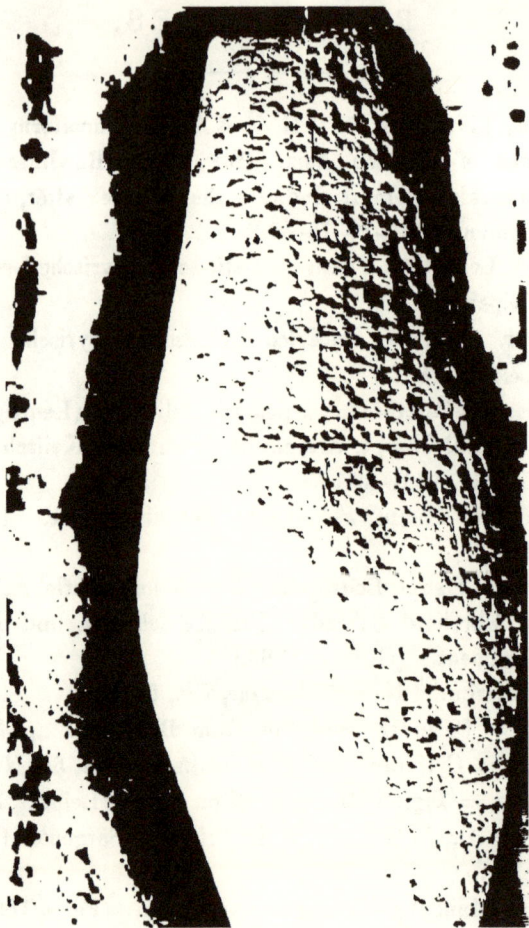

INTRODUCTION.

§ 1.

Having learned that a collection of cuneiform inscriptions had arrived at the Metropolitan Museum of Art, New York, I visited the Museum during the month of August, 1884, to examine the new collection and to practice copying the cuneiform contract tablets at the east end of the building.

Among the valuable pieces of the new collection was a cuneiform Babylonian Cylinder. Upon expressing a wish to copy it, I was informed it could be done only on two conditions. The first was the permission of General L. P. di Cesnola, Director of the Museum; the second was the permission of the owner of the collection, as it was not yet Museum property. With kindly courtesy, facility for study and the privilege of copying the Cylinder was granted by the Director of the Museum. Mr. Bernard Maimon, the actual owner and original collector, also consented with the restriction that no publication should be made until the purchase of the Cylinder by the Museum.

I began my work of copying the inscription in the Museum on August 27th, and completed it during the first week of September.

On October 7th, a communication was sent to me, by the Director's orders, that the Cylinder was now Museum property and the publication open to me, but no restrictions would be placed on any one, and a cast would be forwarded as soon as possible. Towards the end of October I received a cast of the Cylinder,

7

with a note stating that the first one made was forwarded to me according to promise. After taking precautions to be assured that the text was as perfect as could be under the circumstances, the translation was announced on November 17th. With the full text in hand, I began the work of translation and collation with other Babylonian texts, and towards the end of December the work was completed.

The writer takes this occasion of thanking warmly General di Cesnola, Director of the Museum, for that courtesy which he has always extended to students. He acknowledges, with gratitude, his obligations to Prof. Paul Haupt, of the Johns Hopkins University, Baltimore, for many kindnesses and valuable assistance. He is indebted, also, to the kindness of the Rev. J. N. Strassmaier, S. J., London, Eng., for the completed and autographed text here published and for direction and encouragement during the work. With the hope that this first work may be improved upon by the efforts of abler scholars, the text and translation are here presented, to be followed by a commentary, already prepared, with parallel passages from the known Cylinders of Nebuchadnezzar, to which will be added a collation with the texts of Erech, Nabonidus, and the Babylonian inscriptions of Liverpool.

§ 2.

One glance at the photograph of the original will suggest a better idea of a Babylonian Cylinder than could be given by many pages of description. These Cylinders, or barrels, are the official documents of the king, and are usually found in the corner-stones of the temples or other public buildings. The Cylinder measures about nine inches in length, five in diameter at the middle and two inches at the ends.

The writing, in the peculiar Babylonian archaic character, is divided into three sections. On the terra-cotta cylinder, a smooth band, unmarked by characters, running from end to end, indicates the beginning of each column. Unlike the Semitic languages, Ethiopic excepted, the Babylonian as well as the Assyrian cuneiform is read, like our English, from left to right.

This particular Cylinder is of interest, less from any new historical fact that it reveals than from its being, as far as known, the first unpublished original that has found its way from that ancient empire of Babylon to the city of New York, there to tell its story of the work of the mighty king, and confirm anew the facts made known by the other inscriptions of this same monarch.

Every new document, whatever its value, is an additional link in the chain that binds us to the history of past nations. The question is often asked, " of what practical use are these inscriptions?" For the Semitic student no answer is required, but it may be worth while for those not professionally interested in these new and important researches to glance at the significance which these discoveries and interpretations bear in the eyes of leading Assyriologists. We have but to look at the works of Delitzsch, Haupt, Schrader, to see how this language, hidden for centuries, now comes forth to help us reconstruct the history of forgotten nations. The results of cuneiform studies have given rise to a literature full of the deepest interest to men of all opinions and pursuits. These studies may be looked upon from a two-fold point of view, that of philology and history; but both have the same end—the practical use of the results of interpretation.

" The excavations of Mesopotamia, during the last few years," says a paper, read before the Philosophical Society of Great Britain, " have been productive of especially good results. Not only has Assyrian grammar and lexicography been enriched by magnificent 'finds' of bilingual and grammatical tablets, but a considerable quantity of history has been made known to us through the discovery of Cylinders which were inscribed during the latter years of the Babylonian empire. They are peculiarly valuable, because they are the productions of those who lived at the time when the events happened which they record." The contract tablets, and the Egibi tablets give an insight into the commercial affairs of Babylon, and reveal their great loan and banking system. Some of these contract tablets, or notes of legal transfer, are now in the New York Museum. (Cfr. E. A. Budge, On Recent Inscrip. of Neb.)

The contract tablets are very numerous, although only a few have been published, and their chief value hitherto has been the use made of them in regard to dates.

Besides chronology, however, they have supplied valuable material for the Assyrian and Babylonian language, and have enabled us to form some idea of the social and commercial relations under the Babylonian Empire. Until the whole collection has been published, it will not be possible to arrive at very satisfactory results. One quite interesting tablet, published in the "Transactions of the Society of Biblical Archæology," dates from the 17th year of Nabonidus—the time when the Prophet Daniel was In the City of Babylon—as that king is identified by Josephus (Antiq. Jud. X. 11) with Balthassar, the last King of Babylon before the Persian conquest by Cyrus and Darius the Mede. (Cfr. Trans. Soc. Bib. Arch., Vol. VII., Part 3.)

The tablet refers to the purchase of a house to be occupied within four years. The money is deposited with a third party, and the owner remains till the time of actual possession by the purchaser. If purchaser and trustee die, the money will nevertheless go to the owner from whom the house was bought. If the heir of the trustee refuses to pay the money, the owner of the house may bring a lawsuit against him, and the decision of the judges will be in favor of the prosecution.

As to the discovery of this Cylinder of Nebuchadnezzar, the writer learned the facts from Mr. Maimon personally, who gave him the following details: Amid the ruins at Aboo Habba, (the site of Sippara, Sepharvaim of the Hebrews, situated between the Euphrates and the Tigris, north of Babylon and southwest of Bagdad), while searching in the ruins and thrusting into them a spear he held in his hand, Mr. Maimon found considerable resistance in the loose rubbish. Working the spear around the object, he found it to be of considerable size, and, upon digging it out, discovered this Cylinder, bearing an inscription in cuneiform characters.

In the collection gathered by Mr. Maimon were many other valuable pieces—in particular several small Cylinders, with archaic characters and curious designs. Concerning these objects, some time later, a communication was made by Prof. Paul Haupt to the Archæological Society of the Johns Hopkins University, Baltimore, with relation to the Chaldean Antiquities, and another regarding the Arabian portion by Dr. A. L. Frothingham. A portion of this collection was purchased by Prof. Marquand, of Princeton.

§ 3.

The name Nebuchadnezzar has been variously explained. It is found in the cuneiform writings as Nabu-kudurri-usur, written also Na-bi-uv-ku-du-ur-ri-u-su-ur, (VR, 34, Col. II, 67). In Hebrew it becomes Nebû-khodr-essôr, and by successive modifications and corruptions is written and spoken Nebu-khad-nessor, Nebuchadnessor. The transition is easy to the German Nebukadnezzar, and the English Nebuchadnezzar. In the Ναβουχοδονόσορ of the Septuagint, we find the origin of Nabuchadonosor. (Ant. Jud. x. 6.) The name has three elements—Nabû "Nebo," kudurru "crown," usur "protect." "Nebo, protect my crown." Others give to the word kudur, the meaning "landmark." (IR, 52, 5 and 6). (Cfr., Schrader KAT, 362). (Fleming, East India Inscription, p. 22,—Budge, Recently Discovered Inscriptions of Nebuchednezzar, p. 3).

The word Nebo, nabû = "to speak," "prophesy," "prophet," appears as a usual element in the names of Babylonian Kings, Nabopolassar, Nabu-pal-usur, "Nebo, protect my son." From them it passed to members of the royal household, as the general Nebu zardan, and even to persons whom the Babylonians held in honor, as the Jewish captive youth Abednego, signifying "servant of Nebo," so named by the feast-master of Nebuchadnezzar, from the Hebrew "Abed," "servant," and "Nebo," which the Jews, either not under-

standing or rejecting through contempt, changed to Nego. (KAT.
p. 429.) This use of the name of the deity in the names of
individuals, appears, as is well known, in the Hebrew names of
the Angels, Mi-chael—who is like God.

This would hardly be the place to give the history of Nebuchadnezzar and his works (cfr. G. Rawlinson, Seven Monarchies,
Fourth Mon., c. VIII, c. VII, note 12, 18); suffice it to say here,
that unlike the Assyrian Kings, Assurbanipal and Sennacherib, who
glory in their battles and conquests, and in the recital thereof, Nebuchadnezzar's chief glory, if we judge from his inscriptions, seems
to be the building and restoring of the temples of his gods.

§ 4.

The temple referred to in the inscription with which we are
concerned, is the temple E Parra, the temple of the Sun at Sippara.
Sippara or Aboo Habba, is situated on the left bank of the
Euphrates, and being one of the earlier cities, the river Euphrates
itself is called the "river of Sippar." The name appears with
varied spelling, Si-par, Si-ip-par, Sip-par, (II R, 13, 26, d.—V R,
23, 29.—II R, 48, 55, a, b), and with and without determinative.

The god of Sippara was Samas, the Sun god. His temple was
called E Parra, the temple of the Sun. Another city sacred to
Samas was Larsa, called in the non-semitic text, *babbar-unu-ki*,
"dwelling of the sun" (I R, 2, No. 111, IV, 4, 3). In Semitic
phonetic spelling it is found La-ar-sa-am-ki. The temple there was
E-babbara. (Neb. Grot. II, 42.) (Cfr., Del. Paradies, p. 223.
Assyr. Stud. Akkad. Gloss, p. 174. Haupt, ASKT. p. 37, No. 41.)

The other temples mentioned in this inscription, E-Saggil and
E-Zida, were erected, the one to Merodach at Babylon, the other
to Nebo at Borsippa, the sister city of Babylon. Both were subse-
quently restored by Nebuchadnezzar.

E-Sag-ila was the "temple of the lofty head," and was also
named "the palace of Heaven and Earth, the dwelling of Bel,
El, and Merodach." (Neb. Borsip. I. 15 *ff.*)

E-Zida, in Assyrian, bîtu kenu, means the "everlasting dwelling."

The name Babylon occurs in many different forms in the Babylonian inscriptions. Commonly it is written KA-dingir-RA = "the gate of god," Bab-ili, Bâbîlu ; ka, being the Akkadian for "gate," and dingir, the ideogram for "god." (IV R, 12, 13.) The oldest non-semitic form appears as Tintir. (IV R. 20, 3.) We find the name of the city as a pure ideogram : (a) Ka-dingir-(-ra)(ki), (Khors, 2, 6. I R, 48, No. 5, 3); (b) as a phonogram : Ba-bi-lu(ki), (I R, 52, No. 5); (c) as combined ideogram and phonogram : Ba-bi-dingir, i. e. Ba-bi-ilu, (Neb., IV, 28). (Cfr. Del. Paradies., p. 212. Schrader, KAT., p. 121.) Babylon is the Greek form of Babel or Bab-ili, and Ba-bel is the semitic translation of the Akkadian KA-dingir-RA.

Instead of the Assyrian ilu, in Babylonian we read dingir; thus ilu-šu, his god, becomes dingir-na; abu-šu, his father, adda-na. The syllable ra suffixed takes the meaning, " to," " for," as adda-na-ra = to his father. Ka-dingir-ra = the gate to god. (Cfr. Haupt, SFG., p. 3.)

The passages where this name occurs are endless, thus: ina ka-dingir-ra epuš. (IR, Neb., IV Col., l. 17 ; VI Col., l. 26, 29 ; VII Col., ll. 1, 4, 34, 40.)

Again : ina Babili epuš. (IR, Neb., IV, 28, 31.) Bab-ilu and Si-par are both found in the Syllabary. (II R. 13, 25.)

Nebuchadnezzer, son of Nabopolassar, reigned in Babylon from about B. C. 604 to B. C. 560. The first king of Babylon was Nobonassar, B. C. 747. The last was Nabonidus, B. C. 555, who reigned 17 years until the time of Cyrus.

According to the Babylonian canon of Ptolemy, the first year of Nebuchadnezzar's reign is placed at 604 B. C., his father Nabopolassar's at 625, and that of Evil-Merodach, 561. (Cfr. KAT., Schrader, p. 490.)

These observations are deemed sufficient for the understanding of the meaning of the inscription.

The substance of the inscription is as follows :

I am Nebuchadnezzar, King of Babylon, lawful son of Napolassar. I the King of righteousness, the interpreter, the spoiler, filled with the fear of the gods and loving justice, have placed in the hearts of my people the spirit of reverence towards the gods, and as a devout worshipper, have rebuilt their temples E Saggil and E Zida.

This proclamation we issue:

My great Lord Merodach singled me out as the restorer of the city and the rebuilder of its temples, and made my name illustrious.

This proclamation we make:

The temple E Parra, the temple of Samas, which is at Sippara, and which long before my reign, had fallen to ruins, I rebuilt.

The great god Samas, hearkened to no king before me, and gave no command to do this work. But I, his servant, filled with awe of his divinity, in piety and wisdom built his temples, at his inspiration.

I lifted up my hands in constant prayer, for the building of his temple E Parra. The God Samas accepted the lifting up of my hands, he heard my prayer for the building of his temple. Samas, Ramanu and Merodach heard me. My prayer was heard by Samas my Lord, the judge of Heaven and Earth, the warlike, the great hero, the supreme, the glorious Lord, who governs the decisions of justice. The temple of my great Lord, the temple of Parra, at Sippara, in joy and jubilant exultation I built.

O great god Samas, when thou dost enter in joy into the work made by my hands, grant that it may be lasting; look with favor upon me, and may I receive a blessing from thy lips.

Let me sate myself with glory, and grant me a long life and the establishment of my kingdom forever. Let me be an everlasting ruler, with a righteous sceptre, true power, governing my people in peace and prosperity for ever.

By the power of my arms, give success to my warriors in battle; send me, O Samas, prosperous omens—peace and prosperity, and let my arms disperse the power of mine enemies.

15

§ 5.

In the cuneiform text as here given, the lines marked with the numerals are the copy of the Archaic Babylonian, the original text of the Cylinder. The lines marked *b.* are the transcription, character for character of the old Babylonian into the later Babylonian of the sixth century B. C. The lines marked *a.* are the Assyrian characters of the seventh century B. C., as we find them in the inscriptions of the Assyrian kings.

Thus, the triple text may serve as a useful reference for the study and comparison of the Babylonian and Assyrian characters.

In the transcription, the method has been to keep as closely as possible to the syllabication of the Original. The marked letters in the transcription have the usual values of the corresponding letters in Hebrew:

$$\check{s} = sh, \quad s = ts, \quad \underline{h} = ch \; hard, \quad t = teth, \quad k = koph.$$

The work upon the inscription has been done in the intervals of other serious study, and if it be allowed "*parva componere magnis*" the writer would conclude in the words of Frederick Delitzsch in his introduction to the *Paradies.* "It was a difficult work, difficult in itself, and much more difficult from external circumstances; and now that I have reached the end, and look back, there arise before me many defects . . . which are pardonable, indeed, but still remain imperfections. Nevertheless, in the rough ore brought with patience from the depth of the mine, some pure metal may be found. May the science of Archæology and, especially, Biblical science, sift this out; may they make subservient to their advancement, that wide field and promising perspective of language, culture and religion which has been opened to them by the researches of Assyriology."

WOODSTOCK, January, 1885.

Cylinder of Nebukadnezzar at New York.

Col. I. 1. 𒀭𒈾𒁀 ...

b. ...

a. ...

2. ...

b. ...

a. ...

3. ...

b. ...

a. ...

4. ...

b. ...

a. ...

5. ...

b. ...

a. ...

6. ...

b. ...

a. ...

7. ...

b. ...

a. ...

8. ...

b. ...

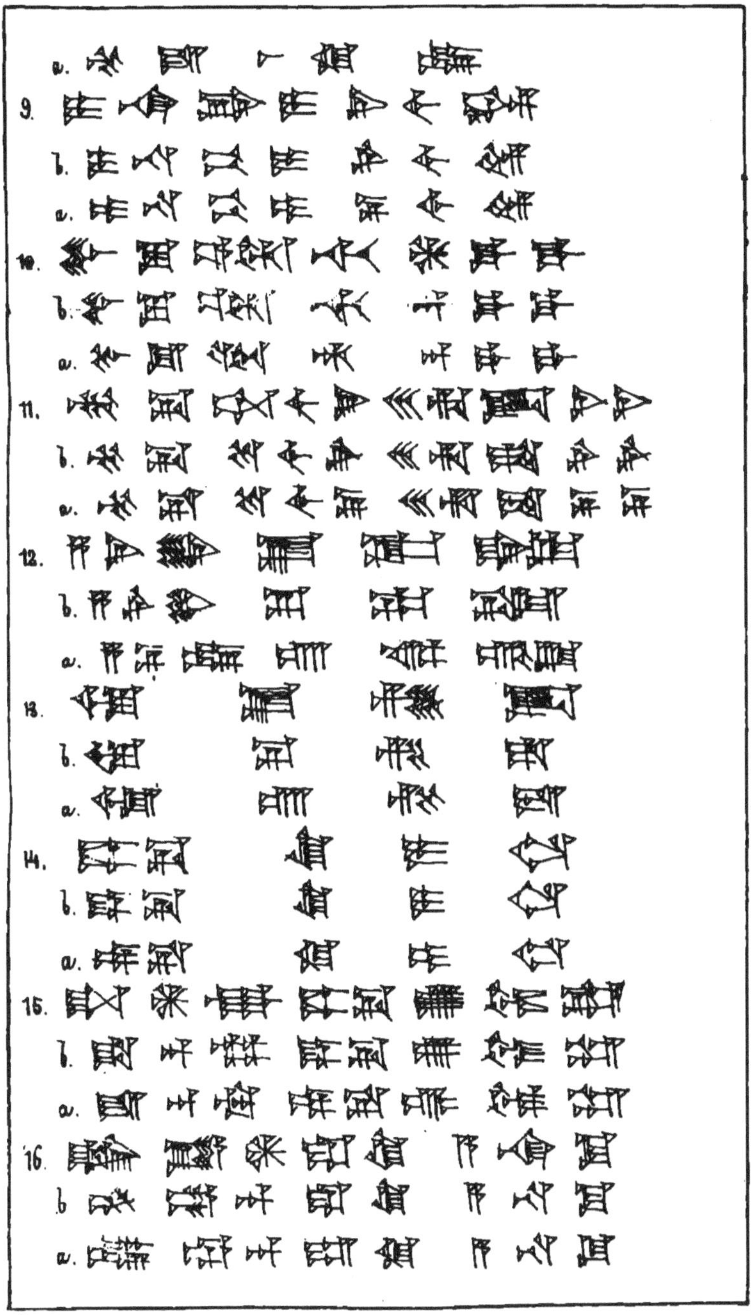
a.
9.
b.
a.
10.
b.
a.
11.
b.
a.
12.
b.
a.
13.
b.
a.
14.
b.
a.
15.
b.
a.
16.
b
a.

2.

17.

b.

a.

18.

b.

a.

19.

b.

a.

20.

b.

a.

21.

b.

a.

22.

b.

a.

23.

b.

a.

24.

b.

a.

25.

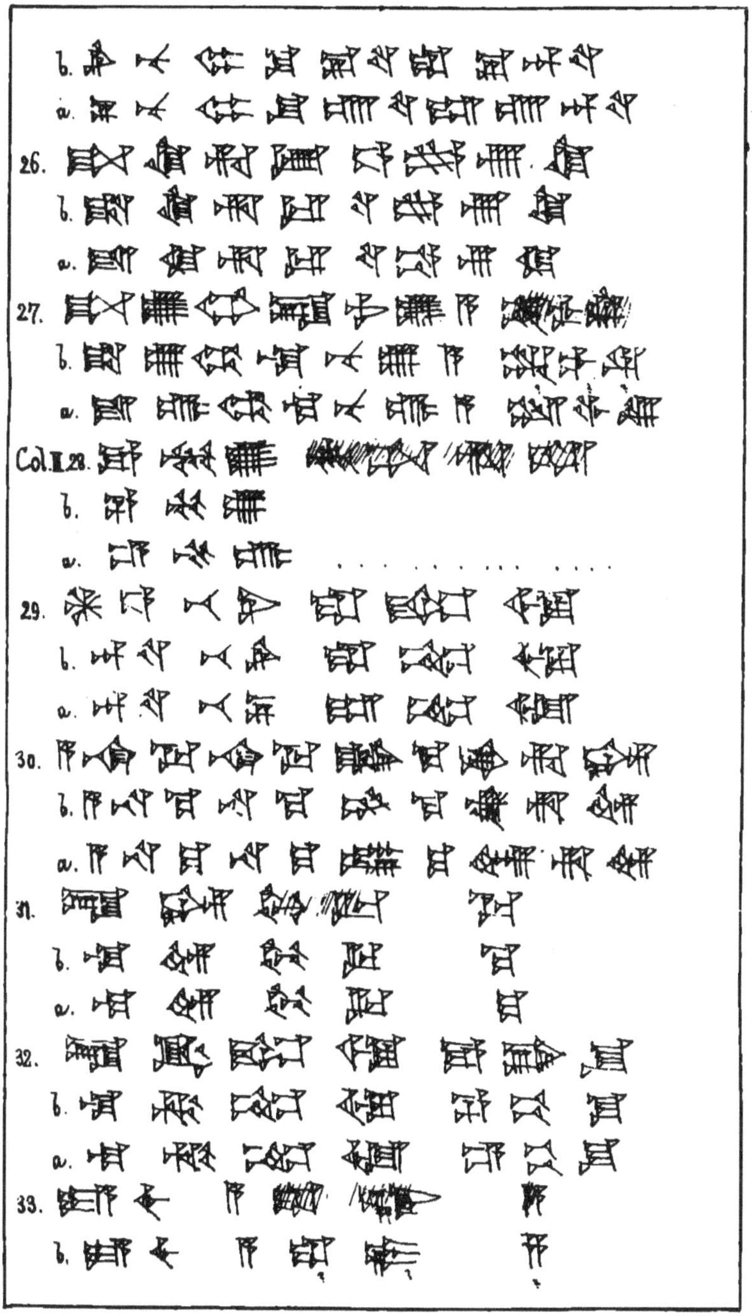
b.
a.
26.
b.
a.
27.
b.
a.
Col.II 28.
b.
a.
29.
b.
a.
30.
b.
a.
31.
b.
a.
32.
b.
a.
33.
b.

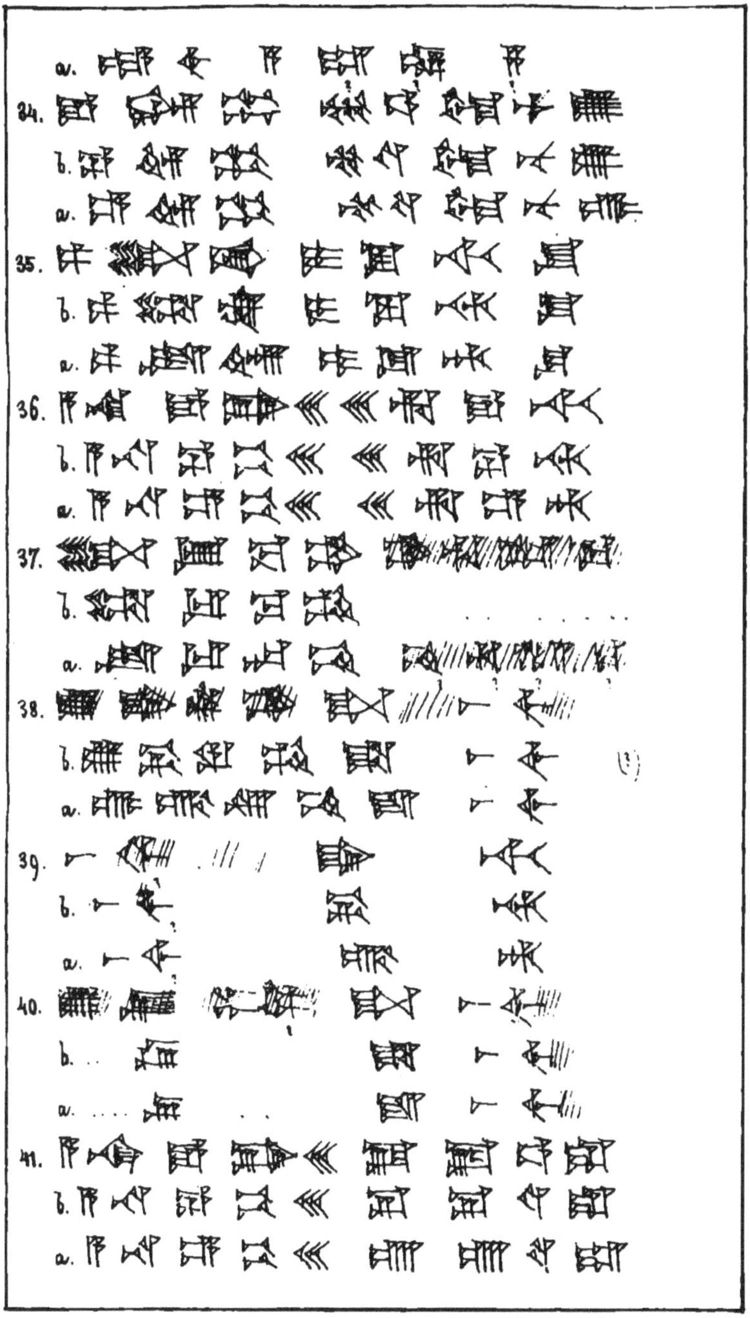
a.
34.
b.
a.
35.
b.
a.
36.
b.
a.
37.
b.
a.
38.
b.
a.
39.
b.
a.
40.
b.
a.
41.
b.
a.

42.
l.
a.
43.
l.
a.
44.
l.
a.
45.
l.
a.
46.
l.
a.
47.
l. ...
a. ...
48.
l.
a.
49.
l.
a.
50.

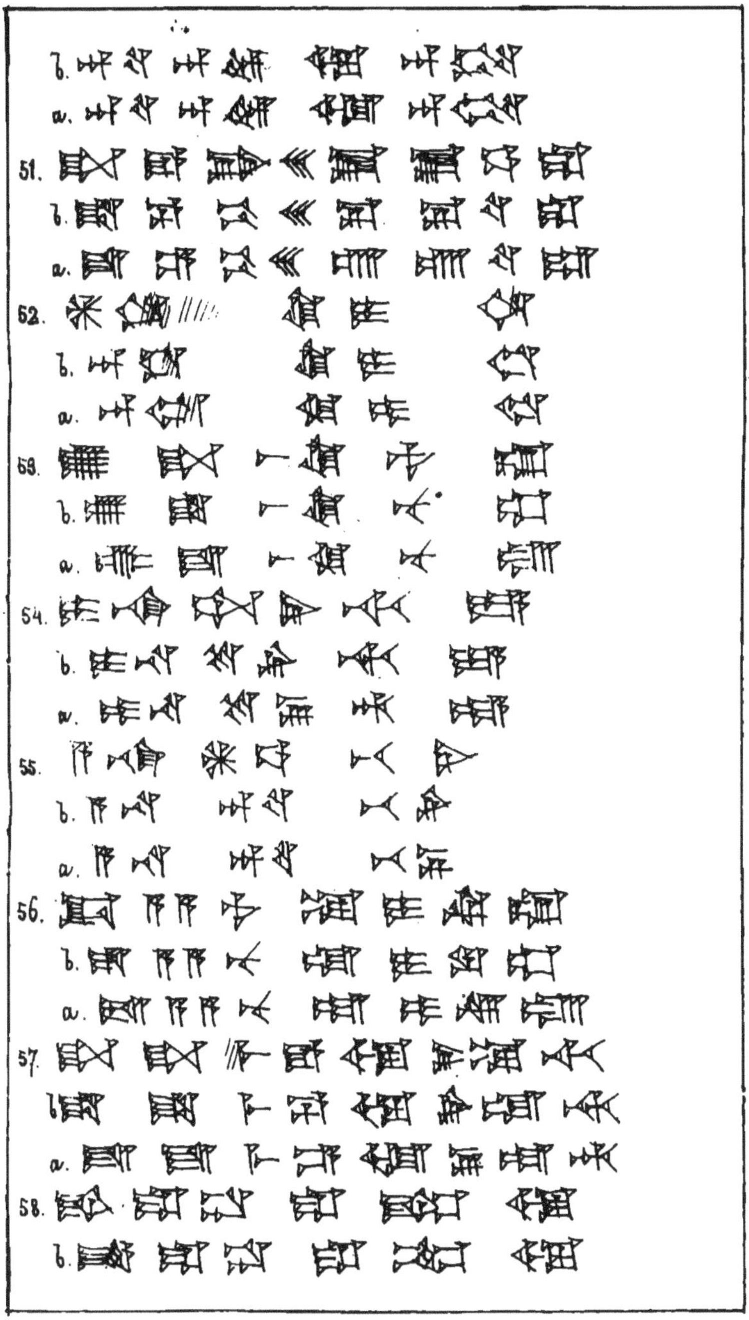
b.
a.
51.
b.
a.
52.
b.
a.
53.
b.
a.
54.
b.
a.
55.
b.
a.
56.
b.
a.
57.
b
a.
58.
b.

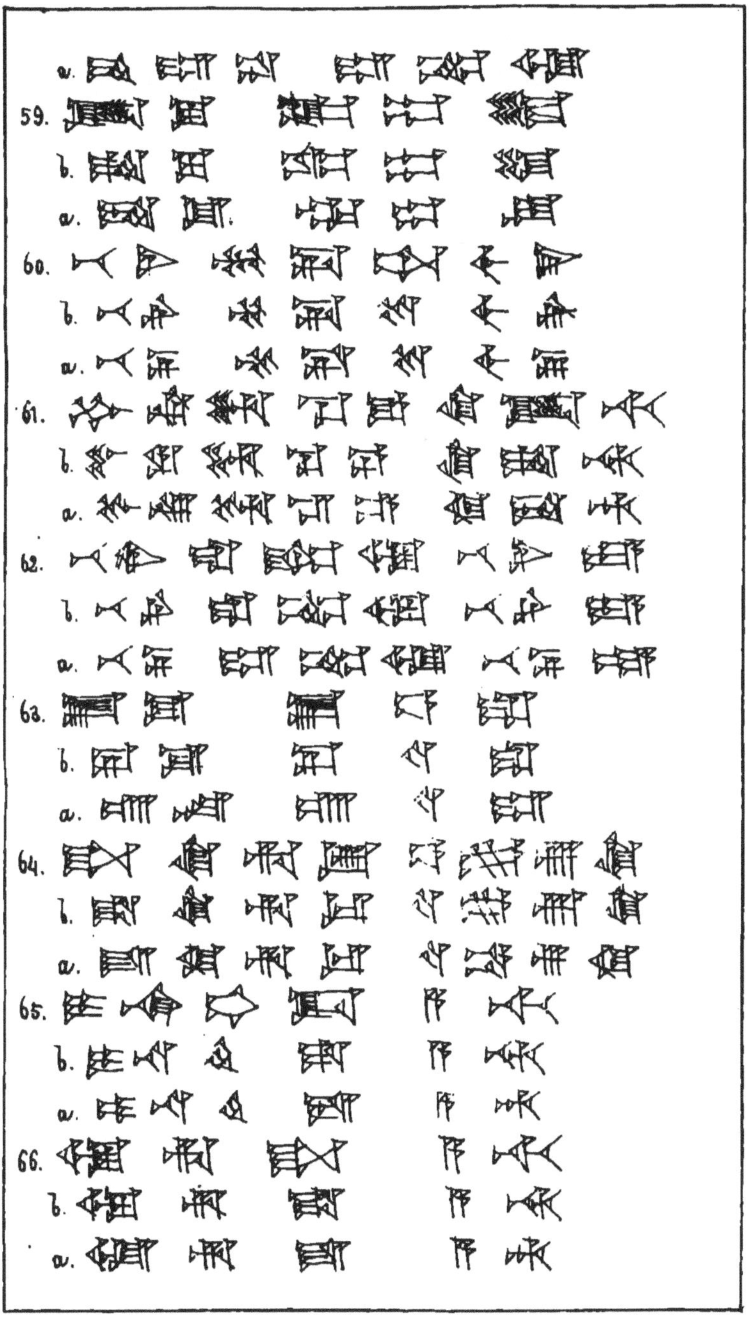
a.
59.
b.
a.
60.
b.
a.
61.
b.
a.
62.
b.
a.
63.
b.
a.
64.
b.
a.
65.
b.
a.
66.
b.
a.

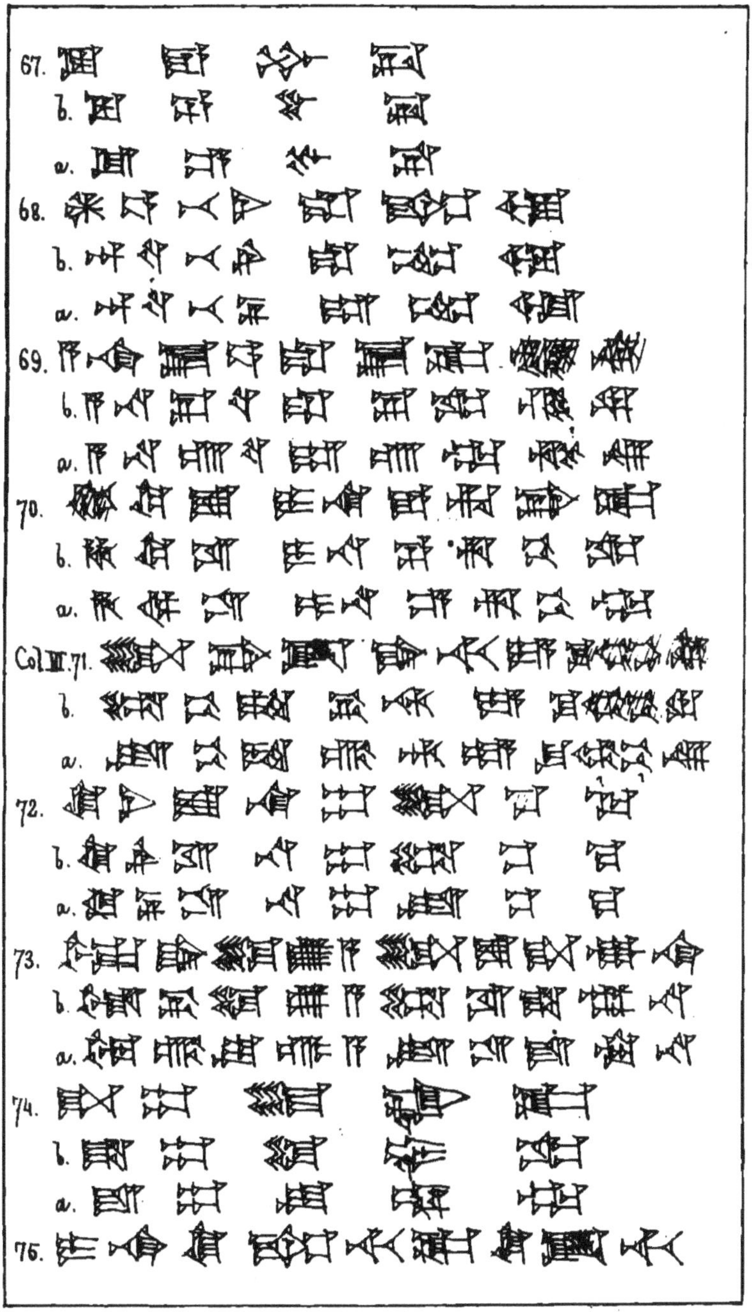
67.
b.
a.
68.
b.
a.
69.
b.
a.
70.
b.
a.
Col. III. 71.
b.
a.
72.
b.
a.
73.
b.
a.
74.
b.
a.
75.

84.
85.
86.
87.
88.
89.
90.
91.

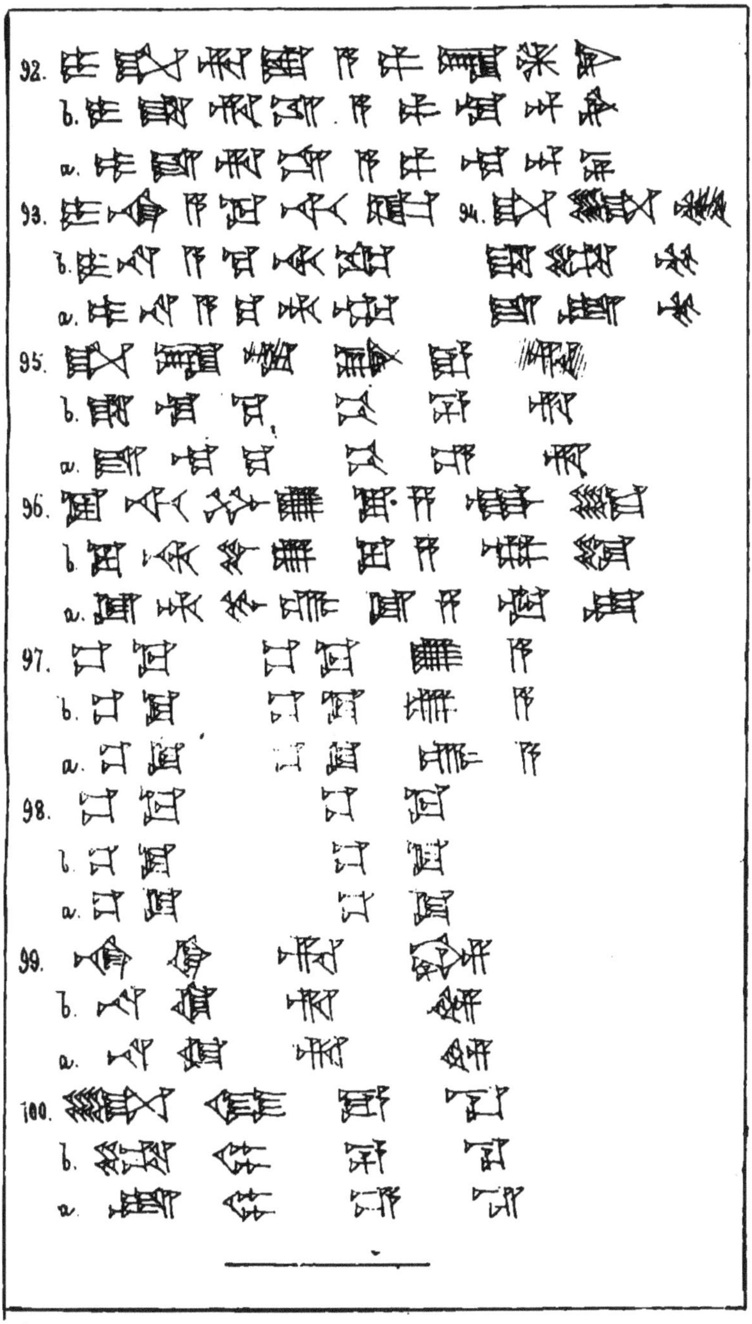
92.
b.
a.
93.
94.
b.
a.
95.
b.
a.
96.
b.
a.
97.
b.
a.
98.
b.
a.
99.
b.
a.
100.
b.
a.

AND

TRANSLATION.

Col. I. 1. Nabû - ku - dur - ru - u - su - ur

šar mi - ša - ri - im

pa - aš - ru, ša - ah - tu

ša pa - la - ah ilâni mu - du - u

5. ra - ' - im ki - it - ti

u mi - ša - ri - im,

mu - uš - te - ' - u ba - la - tam

mu - ša - aš - ki - in

ina bi - i ni - ši - im

10. pu - lu - uh - ti ilâni rabûti

mu - uš - te - ši - ir eš - ri - it ilâni

za - ni - in E - Sag - gil

u E - Zida

aplu ki - i - num

15. ša Nabû - pal - u - su - ur

Šar Bâbîli a - na - ku

Col. I. 1. Nebuchadnezzar,

King of righteousness,

master of life and death,

who knoweth the fear of the gods,

5. loving justice

and righteousness;

seeking life,

establishing

in the mouth of the people

10. the fear of the great gods;

seeker of the temple of the god;

restorer of the temple Saggil,

and the temple Zida;

true Son

15. of Nabopolassar

King of Babylon am I.

Ni-nu: il Marduk

belu ra-bi-u

ana be-lu-ut ma-da

20. iš-ša-an-ni-ma

a-na za-nin-nu-ti ma-ha-za

u ud-du-uš eš-ri-e-ti-šu

šu-ma si-ra-am

ib-bi-u

25. ni-nu-mi-šu E-Parra bit il Šamas

ša ki-ri-ib Sippar

ša u-ul-la-nu-a . . . . . ?

e-mu-u . . . . ?

Col. II.   il Šamaš en-ni ra-bi-u

30. a-na ma-na-ma šarri ma-ah-ri-im

la im-gu-ur-ma

la ik-bi-u e-bi-šu

â-ši . . . . ?

We (proclaim) : the god Merodach

my great lord

to rule the country

20. raised me up;

for the restoration of the city,

and the renewing of its temples

my lofty name

he gave forth.

25. We (proclaim) this: The temple of Parra,
    the temple of the Sun
    which is in Sippara,

which long before me (had fallen to ruins?)

and decay . . . (I built ?)

Col. II. The god Samas my great lord

30. not to any former King

had he hearkened and

had not commanded to do (this)

1 . . (his servant?)

e - im - ku   mu - ut - nin - nu - u

35. pa - li - iḫ   i - lu - ti - šu

a - na   e - bi - eš   eš - ri - e - ti

li - ib - ba   (uštallit) :

u - ga - ru   am - ša - as - si (?)

aš - ši   ga - ti

40. u - sa - ap - pa - ša   aš - ši (?)

a - na   e - bi - eš   bîti   E - Parra

u - mi - šu   um - ma

Šamaš   en - ni   ra - bi - u

ni - iš   ga - ti - ia   im - ḫu - ur - ma

45. iš - ša - a   su - pi - e - a

a - na   e - bi - eš   bîti   šu - a - ti

e - bi - eš   bîti   ša   il   Šamaš

il   Šamaš   il   Ramânu   u   il   Marduk

ip - ru - us - ma   .   (?)

50. il   Šamaš   il   Ramanu   u   il   Marduk

wise and pious,

35. (was in) fear (of) his divinity.

to build the temples

he (directed) my heart:

I cleared the grounds (?)

I lifted up my hands,

40. and I made supplication (?)

for the building of the temple Parra,

day by day, (to)

the god Samas, my great lord.

the lifting up of my hands he accepted;

45. he received my prayers

for the building of that temple,

the building of the temple of Samas.

Samas, Ramanu and Merodach

turned (?) and (hearkened).

50. Samas, Ramanu and Merodach

ša e - bi - eš bîti E - Parra

an - num (?) ki - i - num

u - ša - aš - ki - nu - um

i - na te - ir - ti - ia

55. a - na il Šamaš en - ni

da - a - a - nu si - i - ru - um

ša ša - me - e u ir - si - ti

kar - ra - du ra - bi - u

it - lu ka - ab - tu . . .

60. be - lu mu - uš - te - ši - ir

pu - ru - us - si - e ki - it - ti

beli ra - bu - u beli - ia

bit - su E - Parra

ša kirib Sipar

65. ina hi - da - a - ti

u ri - ša - a - ti

lu e - pu - uš

for building the temple Parra

true mercy

established

during my reign.

55. Unto Samas, my lord,

the supreme judge

of heaven and earth,

the warlike, the great hero,

the supreme, the glorious lord,

60. the lord who directs

the decision of righteousness,

to the great lord, my lord,

his temple E Parra,

which is in Sippara,

65. in joy

and jubilant exaltation

I built. ,

ilu Šamaš beli rabu - u

a - na E - Parra biti - ka nam - ru

70. ḫa - di - iš i - na e - ri - bi - ka

Col. III.   li - bi - it ga - ti - ia šu - ul - bi - ir

ki - ni - iš na - ap - li - iš - ma

dam - ga - tu - a li - iš - šak - na

ša - ap - tu - uk - ka

75. i - na ki - bi - ti - ka ki - it - ti

lu - uš - ba - ' li - it - tu - ti

ba - la - ṭam ana û - um ru - ku - u - ti

ku - un kussî lu - ṣi - ri - iḳ - tu - um - ma

li - ri - ku li - iš - ša - libu

80. ri - ' - u - u a - na dâra - a - ti

ḫattu i - ša - ar - ti

ri - e - u - ti ṭa - ab - ti

ši - bi - ir - ri ki - i - num

mu - ša - li - im ni - ši

The god Samas, my great lord

into the temple E Parra, thy glorious temple,

70. upon thy joyful entering therein

Col. III.   the brickwork of my hands let it endure.

look with grace, (upon me) and

mercy, may it (be) established (by)

thy word (lip).

75. by thy righteous command,

let me sate myself with glory ;

life unto days remote

stability of my throne mayest thou grant.

may they be long (the days of my reign),

80. Lordship for eternity,

a righteous sceptre,

just sway,

true insignia of sovereignty,

prosperity to my people

85. lu - i - ba (?) ḫattu šar - ru - ti - ia

      a - na dâra - a - ti

      i - na kakkê ez - zuti

      te - bu - ti ta - ḫa - za

      lu - zu - lu - ul um - ma - ni - (ia?)

90. il Šamaš atta - ma

      ina di - i - num u bi - i - ri

      i - ša - ri - is a - pa - la - an - ni

      ina a - ma - ti - ka

      ša - li - mu

95. ša - la - ma bi - e - ri

      lu - ti - bu - u lu - za - ak - tu

      kakku kakkua

      kakke

      na - ki - ri - im

100. li - mi - e - si

85. giving peace (?) to the sceptre of my royalty

unto eternity.

with mighty weapons,

with a successful battle

let me adorn my troops.

90. The god Samas thou,

in judgment and oracles,

in righteousness, bind me

in thy word.

grant success,

95. a lasting prosperity.

May they draw near, may they sting,

the weapon; my weapon,

the weapons

of the enemy

100. let it disperse.

www.ingramcontent.com/pod-product-compliance
Lightning Source LLC
Chambersburg PA
CBHW031800090426
42739CB00008B/1102